TERRA VERDE

Dream Independent Press

Siyana S, born in Kerala is a debut poet and nature enthusiast. Her first collection of poetry, "Terra Verde", explores the beauty and wonder of the natural world.She has always been fascinated by the intricate relationships between humans and the environment. Her poetry collection is a reflection of this curiosity.

TERRA VERDE

Siyana

Dream Independent Press

Terra Verde | Siyana S

Published by DREAM INDEPENDENT PRESS

Dream Independent Press is a part of Dream Bookbindery, whose addresses can be found at www.dreambookbindery.com

First Published by Dream Independent Press in 2024

ISBN 9789390800841

Typeset in Garamond by TEAM: MAAYA, Kerala
Cover Design by TEAM: MAAYA

Printed and Bound in India

This book is produced from independently certified FSC® paper to ensure responsible forest management.

FOREWORD

In the depths of our collective unconscious, there lies a primal longing to connect with the natural world. A world that was once our sole domain, where the rhythms of life were dictated by the sun, the moon, and the seasons. Yet, in our increasingly urbanized and technology-driven existence, we find ourselves increasingly disconnected from the land that sustains us.

This poetry collection is a testament to the human desire to reclaim that connection, to rekindle the flame of wonder and awe that burns within us when we gaze upon the majesty of nature. These poems are a celebration of the beauty and diversity of the natural world, from the towering mountains to the quietest streams, from the lush forests to the arid deserts.

Through their words, these poets invite us to step into a world that is both familiar and yet, utterly foreign. A world where the boundaries between species blur, where the lines between human and animal are erased, and where the very essence of existence is distilled into its most elemental form.

As we wander through these pages, we are reminded of the ancient wisdom that lies within us, waiting to be unearthed. We are reminded of the power of nature to heal and transform us, to awaken us to our own humanity and our place within the grand tapestry of life.

This poetry collection is a paean to the beauty and mystery of nature, a declaration of love and reverence for the land that gives us life. It is a reminder that our existence is not separate from the natural world, but an integral part of it – a strand in the intricate web of life that binds us all together.

In these pages, you will find poems that will transport you to distant landscapes, poems that will evoke memories of childhood adventures, poems that will stir your soul and awaken your senses. You will find poems that will make you laugh, cry, and ponder the mysteries of existence.

And as you read through these pages, I hope you will find yourself drawn back into the fold of nature's arms, where you will rediscover your own place within the grand narrative of life.

PREFACE

In the stillness of the forest, where ancient trees stretch towards the sky, and the gentle rustle of leaves whispers secrets to the wind, I find solace. It is here, among the rhythms of nature, that I come alive. For in the intricate dance of earth and sky, I am reminded of the beauty and wonder that lies just beyond our daily grasp.

This collection of poems is a love letter to the natural world, an attempt to capture the essence of the land, sea, and sky that has shaped my own journey. Each poem is a fragment of a larger tapestry, woven from threads of observation, imagination, and introspection. From the towering mountains to the smallest blade of grass, I have sought to distil the essence of nature's majesty, and to convey its power to transform, inspire, and heal.

These poems are not simply a celebration of the beauty of nature; they are also a reflection of our own humanity. For in the natural world, we find echoes of our own hopes, fears, and desires. We see mirrored in its landscapes and creatures our own struggles and triumphs. And in its quiet moments, we are reminded of the preciousness and fragility of life itself.

As I reflect on the natural world, I am reminded that poetry is not just about words on a page; it is about the way we listen to the world around us. It is about tuning in to the rhythms of life, and allowing ourselves to be shaped by their beauty and mystery. And it is with this spirit in mind that I offer these poems to you – as a testament to the transformative power of nature, and as a reminder to slow down, listen deeply, and allow ourselves to be inspired by the beauty that surrounds us.

ACKNOWLEDGEMENT

I would like to acknowledge the incredible inspiration and guidance that my poetry collection, "Terra Verde", has received from the Muses themselves. Your whispers in my ear have been the catalyst for the words that flow onto the page.

I would like to acknowledge the incredible poetry community that has nurtured and inspired me throughout my journey. From open mic nights to writing workshops, you have all been a source of motivation and guidance. Your passion and creativity are a constant reminder of why I write.

I would like to thank my editor, for their tireless efforts in helping me shape this collection into its current form. Your keen eye and insightful feedback have been invaluable in helping me refine my craft.

I would like to extend my heartfelt gratitude to my family and friends, who have supported me throughout my journey.

I would like to acknowledge the readers who have taken the time to immerse themselves in my poetry. Your engagement and feedback have been a source of joy and inspiration, and I am grateful for the opportunity to share my work with you.

I would like to acknowledge the countless hours of writing, editing, and rewriting that have gone into this collection. It has been a labour of love, and I am proud of the final product. Thank you for believing in yourself and your art.

DEDICATION

"To the beauty of impermanence, and to the fleeting moments that make life worth savouring."

PART 1

I

Remembering the days of yore,
I could discern a teenybopper;
Who sat in the midst of the huge valley of florets,
"Those blubbering bells",
Were they sayin something? Nay
Some singing sandies; they too were yelling.
Towards me;
Neither mattered nor I cared.
The reddish eye made them shut their creaks,
Then they exchanged the messages with their chants;
Fresh as the sandal trees'
Dusks made them elegant,
For them it was a bidding farewell.
"And for now, where are the bells, the sands and the blossoms"; couldn't see anyone,
Instead a new window opened before me,
I saw the same teenybopper transform into an old one,
"Yelling for the valley to be seen again".

II

Deep array of sunshine surrounds me,
A delightful, magical setting it is.
The trees; they're enormous and broad, and the soft rustle of their leaves embraces me.
Down the valley,
The sunbeams are busy casting a warm glow that makes everything seem joyful and radiant.
The blooms appear all around,
A spectrum of hues, for both you and me.
Looking away,
Brilliant rays are flying high and high with their brilliant plumes aglow.
The tiny yellow whistles in chatter as they pass,
Gathering nectar from the drum of each flower.
A short gaze away,
I heard the brook murmuring,
And, the sky casts an image, like a glittering dream.
I see old rocks telling stories of a mysterious spot.
Such a mysterious spot exist!
I wonder.
Zephyr whispers can be heard too,
It is the secrets of distant locations and treasured adventures.
The clouds drift by, with such strong outlines.
A chameleon's game where creativity is used.
A treasure trove of a child's heart to discover!

III

Florets, so pretty and bright,
Why do you have to wilt and fade tonight?
I saw you the day before, all fresh and new,
Droopiness haunts you today!
Like my favourite shoe.
They say it's natural, that all things must end,
Chimerical it is!
Yet to believe.
To make them last forever, just for me?
I want to keep them pretty, wild and free.
I remember when you first came to our door,
A bouquet of colours,
A sweet surprise in store.
I danced around my world,
Ecstatic I was!
Wrapped by your petals and stems,
Delightful it was!
But now you touches the feet of mortality.
And I'm left with memories, of what we used to do.
I'll hold on tight to the memories I made,
Of the beauty we shared, before you started to fade.
They say it's okay, it's just part of life,
But I don't want to let go,
Of your sweet, sweet strife.
I'll hold on to your beauty, in my heart and mind,
And cherish the time we had, before you said goodbye.
Oh, florets, oh so fleeting and bright,
Why do you have to go, without a fight?
I'll keep your memory alive, in my dreams and play,
And hope that someday, you'll come back to stay.

IV

I wander through the forest, hand in hand with my dad,
Where trees are taller than houses, and flowers bloom in every pad.
But as I look around, I notice something strange and sad,
The trees are dying, like grandpas, with their leaves all gone bad.

"Why are they all so brown?" I ask my dad with a frown.
"Is it because they're old? Like grandma's rocking chair?"
He nods and says, "Yes, child, it's true. They grow and decay,
Like everything in nature. Nothing stays forever the same way."

I look at the flowers, once so bright and full of cheer,
Now wilted and dry, like grandma's hair when she's old and grey.
"What happens to them?" I ask, my voice full of dismay.
"Where do they go when they're gone?"

My dad takes a deep breath, and his eyes get all misty.
"Well, child, it's a big secret. But I'll tell you what I know.
When they die, their bodies go back to the earth below,
And their energy goes up to the sky, like a bird in flight."

I think about this for a moment, trying to understand.
It's like when my pet fishy dies, and I have to say goodbye.
But then I see the new flowers blooming, all colorful and bright,
And I realize that death is just a part of life's big light.

I look up at my dad, and he's smiling at me.
"You're growing up, kiddo. You're starting to see."
The world is full of secrets, and some are hard to bear,
But with love and family, we can face them all with care.

V

In the forest, where we play,
Stands a tree, with branches grey.
It's been here, for as long as me,
A constant friend, for you and me.
Its bark is rough, its leaves are green,
But I see something, that's unseen.
It's tired, like grandma, old and gray,
Its limbs are weak, its roots astray.
I see the cracks, where water flows,
The scars, where bugs and worms go.
The wind whispers secrets, in its ear,
Of storms that came, and summers dear.
But still it stands, through rain and snow,
A sentinel, for all to know.
It's seen the seasons, ebb and flow,
And told the stories, only trees can show.
I wonder when, its final stand,
Will come to pass, in this land.
Will I be there, when it falls to ground?
And if so, what will I find around?
I'll visit often, while I can,
And listen close, to its ancient plan.
For though it's mortal, like us all,
This tree's wisdom, will forever stand tall.

VI

Huge rocks surround me,
Tall and grand,
Their peaks reaching for the sky so wide.
My parents say they've been around since the land,
But I don't know how much longer they'll stay inside.

Sometimes I think about what they'll do when they're gone,
When their rocks and stones are all that remain.
Will they become just a memory, like a song?
Or will they fade away like a sunset's flame?

My parents tell me stories of their ancient might,
Of how they stood strong through the darkest night.
But even the strongest things can fall and fade,
And leave behind just a memory, a worn-out shade.

I wish I could keep them young and new,
But time is passing, and it's something we can't do.
I'll try to remember every peak and every slope,
And cherish the time I have to watch them grow.

But for now, I'll stand and gaze at their height,
And try to hold onto their beauty, shining bright.
For though they're mortal, and will one day be gone,
They'll always be in my heart, a memory that's strong.

VII

Petioles! are falling down,
Like golden rain, all around.
They crunch beneath my feet so bright,
A treasure trove, a wondrous sight.
I watch them spin, and twirl, and sway,
In the breeze, they dance and play.
But Mama says, with a gentle sigh,
They won't stay here, they'll say goodbye.
What do you mean? I don't understand,
Why would they leave this magical land?
I want them to stay, to colour the ground,
To make the world a more vibrant sound.
But Mama whispers secrets in my ear,
That life is fleeting, and death is near.
They are old, their time is done,
And winter's chill will soon be won.
I look at them, with tears in my eyes,
As they rustle away, and reach the skies.
I wish I could hold them tight,
And keep their beauty, shining bright.
But even I know, that's not the way,
For life is precious, and fleeting each day.
The leaves will fall, and we'll make new friends,
And in the cycle of life, it will begin again.
So, I'll hold on tight, to this autumn's gleam,
And cherish the memories, of this fleeting dream.
For though the leaves may fall, and fade away,
Their beauty will linger, in my heart each day.

VIII

Brook, you're so free and wild,
A ribbon of water, winding mild.
You babble and chirp, and splash with glee,
A symphony of joy, for you and me.
But sometimes, when the sun is high,
I see your edges, starting to dry.
Your waters shrink, your banks grow wide,
And I feel a pang, deep inside.
Why do you dwindle, dear brook of mine?
Why do you fade away, like a summer's shine?
Do you know how much joy you bring,
To all the creatures, who dance and sing?
I know you're just a brook, a tiny stream,
But to me, you're so much more, a dream.
You remind me to play, to laugh and be free,
And I'll miss you dearly, when you're gone from me.
But even in death, I know you'll live on,
In the memories we made, beneath your sunny dawn.
Your ripples will stay, in my heart's pool,
And I'll remember the joy, we had in your cool.
So rest now, dear brook, and let your waters sleep,
For I'll come back to visit, and remember the fun we kept.
And though you may fade away from sight,
In my heart, your song will shine so bright.

IX

A fleeting friend!, who never stays inside.
It whispers secrets, in my ear so fine,
Of distant lands, and memories divine.
But soon, it's gone, and I'm left to sigh,
For I've learned that wind can't stay and fly.
It's like a dream, that slips away at night,
Leaving me with tears, and a heart in flight.
Why does it come, with gentle breeze,
Only to vanish, with whispers of pleas?
Is it seeking solace, in a world so vast,
A moment's peace, before its final pass?
I see it dancing, through leaves so bright,
A waltz of wonder, in the morning light.
But as I watch, it starts to fade away,
Like the dying breath, of a summer's day.
Oh, wind, dear wind, don't leave me so,
For I've grown to love, your gentle flow.
Though you're mortal, and must depart,
Your whispers stay, in my heart.
For now, I'll hold on tight to your sighs,
And cherish every moment, of your windy surprise.
And though you'll leave me soon, to wander free,
Your memory will stay, in my childhood's glee.

X

In fleeting whispers, it arrives,
A gentle caress, a warm surprise.
The sun's soft touch, a precious gift,
A moment's joy, before it shifts.
Its rays dance, like diamonds bright,
Across the earth, in morning light.
But soon, alas, its journey ends,
And with each day, its power descends.
Like autumn's leaves, its vigour wanes,
Its golden glow, a fading stain.
It struggles on, through clouded skies,
Yet even its will, begins to sigh.
In twilight's hush, its final beam,
Fades like a sigh, a whispered dream.
And darkness claims, its sacred right,
The mortal sun, in endless night.
Yet even in its passing breath,
Lies beauty, truth, and life's great death.
For in its fleeting light, we find
The value of each moment's design.
So let us cherish every ray,
And make each moment count, each day.
For in the sun's mortality, we see
A reflection of our own mortality.

XI

In granite's steadfast heart, a truth I've found
A "mortal crown"
For stones, like all, must face their end
Their beauty, fragile, will descend
Like tears of time, they slowly wear
Their surfaces, once smooth, now rough and rare
Their colours, once vibrant, now fade to grey
As they succumb to the ravages of day
Their strength, once unyielding, now begins
To crumble, crack, and disintegrate within
Their bonds, once strong, now break and sever
As they succumb to the relentless heaver
Of wind and rain, of earth and sun
Their final whispers, their eternal done
Their silence, once a testament to age
Now echoes through the void of their stage
And yet, in death, they find a peace
Their beauty lost, their memories released
Their stories told, their secrets kept
In the dust that remains, their legacy slept
So let us cherish these stones so dear
For though they wither, they hold us near
In their mortality, we find our own
A fleeting life, a beauty grown.

XII

Born of mountain's kiss,
Dances down, with life's brief bliss.
It rises high, with vigor and might,
And flows with purpose, through morning's light.
Its waters sparkle, like diamonds bright,
Reflecting sunbeams, with all its might.
It whispers secrets, to the forest deep,
As it weaves its path, in endless sleep.
But like all life, it's mortal and brief,
A moment's joy, a lifetime's grief.
It slows its pace, as it reaches the plain,
And finally rests, in a weary refrain.

The ripples cease, the flow subsides,
The stream's life force, with the tides.
The forest mourns, its fleeting friend,
As the stream's mortality, comes to an end.
Yet in its memory, a tale is told,
Of life's transience, young and old.
For though it's gone, its legacy remains,
In the echoes of its life-giving streams.
And though it's silent, its song remains,
In the hearts of those who knew its name.
For in its fleeting beauty, we're reminded too,
Of the preciousness of life, and all we can do.

XIII

The sky is crying, Mommy says
The clouds are weeping, they're grey and grey
The sun is hiding, it's hard to play
I'm scared, I don't know what's going away

I look up high, and all I see
Is a big old blanket, all grey and sea
It's like the sky is dying, it's true
I miss the blue, I miss the sun shining through

I want my sky back, I want it bright
I want to play outside, day and night
I want to see the stars twinkling high
But now it's just a big ol' cloudy sky

Mommy says it's just a phase
The sun will come back, in a little while it'll gaze
But I'm scared, I don't know what's to come
I just want my sky back, my happy home

The sky is crying, Mommy says
The clouds are weeping, they're grey and grey
But I'll hold on tight, to her hand
And wait for the sun to come back to our land.

XIV

Pieces of nuggets, so strong,
A piece of earth, been here so long.
It's sturdy and rough, with edges sharp,
A piece of nature's endless art.
I wonder if this rock will last,
Through time and seasons moving fast.
Will it crumble, fade away,
Or stand strong like it does today?
I see it weathered, worn with age,
A silent story on its face.
It's been here before I was born,
And will remain long after I'm gone.

I think about its mortality,
How even rocks face finality.
It makes me sad, this truth I know,
That everything had its time to go.
But as I hold it in my hand,
I feel a sense of wonder and,
I realize that in its dust,
The rock lives on, a part of us.
So I'll cherish this rock, cradle it tight,
And marvel at its endless fight.
For though it may not last forever,
Its memory will leave me never.

XV

Water, oh water, so clear and so bright,
You're always there, day and night.
In the river, you flow and play,
And bring life to the world in every way.
But sometimes, I see you go away,
Dry up, and disappear from sight.
The plants get all wilted and grey,
And the animals search for you in vain.
I don't understand why you must leave,
Why you must die, and cease to be.
You're like a friend, so dear and true,
But like all things, you're mortal too.
I know that you're part of the cycle,
Of life and death, and rebirth's wheel.
You evaporate, and rise to the sky,
And then come back down, as rain or dew to dry.
But even though I know this is true,
It's hard for me to see you go away from me too.
I'll miss you, dear water, while you're gone,
And hope that you'll return soon, strong.
So here's a poem to you, dear water,
A poem to remember you by.
You may be gone, but I'll never forget,
The joy and life you brought to my feet.
I'll cherish every moment we had,
And hope that someday, we'll be together again, glad.
For though you're mortal, I know you're true,
And I'll always remember you, dear water, anew.

PART II

I

In the quiet of the forest deep,
Where ancient trees their secrets keep,
I find solace in the timeless rhythm,
Of nature's everlasting kingdom.

The streams that flow, the birds that sing,
They have seen empires rise and fall,
Yet they remain, untouched by time's cruel sting,
A testament to nature's lasting thrall.

The mountains stand tall, their peaks untouched,
By human hands or fleeting thoughts,
They bear witness to the ages past,
A reminder that nature's beauty lasts.

The flowers bloom, the seasons change,
But the essence of nature remains the same,
It is a comfort in a world so strange,
A constant in a world of fleeting fame.

So let me find my peace in the embrace,
Of nature's everlasting grace,
For in its immortality I find my place,
A reminder of life's eternal embrace.

II

In gardens of youth, where petals play,
A fleeting beauty, that's here to stay.
For in their brief life, they bloom with might,
And in their death, they leave a lingering light.

But as I stand, with age's weight upon,
I see the flowers, in a different tone.
Their immortality, now a wistful sigh,
For though they bloom, they will not deny.

Their lives a spark, that flickers bright and bold,
But soon extinguished, leaving naught but cold.
Yet in their passing, a lesson I've gained,
That life's brevity, is the only thing sustained.

For though they may not live on forevermore,
Their memory stays, and their beauty's score.
In the hearts of those who've seen them grow,
Their essence lives on, as the seasons go.

And so I'll cherish, these fleeting things,
These flowers that bloom, and then take wing.
For in their transience, I find a peace,
That comes from knowing, their beauty will release.

III

As I stand beneath your boughs, I ponder on your fame,
The whispers of the ages, etched upon your name.
You've seen the rise and fall of empires, civilizations too,
And yet, you remain, a testament to time's decree.

Your roots delve deep into the earth, your branches stretch to sky,
Unmoving, steadfast, while the world around you passes by.
You've weathered storms and seasons, droughts and heat and cold,
Enduring all, a constant presence, young and old.

Your bark is worn and wrinkled, like the lines on my face,
A map of memories, stories untold, in every place.
You've watched as generations grew, as families came and went,
As lovers strolled beneath your shade, and children laughed and bent.

You've seen the beauty of the world, in all its forms and hues,
And yet, you've stood unmoved, a symbol of eternal truth.
For in your stillness, I find solace, a sense of peaceful rest,
A reminder that some things endure, even when all else is lost.

Your immortality is a mystery, a gift from above,
A connection to the earth, a bond that's strong and true.
You are the guardians of our memories, our hopes and fears,
A living bridge between past and present, through all the passing years.

As I stand beneath your boughs, I am reminded of my own,
Mortality's fleeting grasp, a whisper in my ear.
But you, dear tree, are timeless, a reminder of what's true,
A symbol of endurance, a gift from heaven to me and you.

IV

The leaves that rustle, fade and fall,
A fleeting life, a seasonal call.
But as I stand, a weathered soul,
I see the truth, beyond the role.
For in their whispers, I hear a tale,
Of immortality, without a fail.
For though they wither, shrink and grey,
Their essence lives, in a new way.
In seed and stem, their legacy stays,
A promise kept, through endless days.
Their wisdom grown, through sun and rain,
Echoes of a life that's not in vain.
As I reflect, on life's brief span,
I see the leaves, in a different clan.
Their cycles, like our own design,
A dance of life, in an endless line.
Their stories told, in every hue,
Of trials faced, and lessons anew.
Their resilience, a lesson true,
To weather time, and see it through.
So as I gaze, on autumn's fade,
I'm reminded of the leaves' parade.
For though they fall, their tale remains,
A testament to eternal reign.
Their immortality, a mystery deep,
A secret kept, in their eternal sleep.
And as I stand, beneath their shade,
I'm filled with awe, at their life displayed.
For in their whispers, I hear my own,
A call to live, beyond the zone.

To weather life's storms, and face the test,
And find the strength, to be at my best.
And so I'll take, this lesson true,
From leaves that wither, yet remain anew.
And find my own path, to immortality's gate,
And join the cycle, of life's eternal state.

V

Flowers of fleeting beauty, born of earth and sun,
Your transience is a fleeting thought, yet in your passing, we've begun,
To cherish the memories, the scent, the colors that remain,
And wonder if perhaps, in some way, you might live on, remain.

Your petals may wither, your stems may fade and bend,
But in our hearts, your essence will forever transcend,
The seasons come and go, and with them, you take flight,
Leaving behind only whispers of your radiant light.

Yet, is it not possible, that in some hidden way,
Your immortal soul, a spark of life, remains to stay?
A seed that's sown, a promise kept, a legacy to bear,
A reminder that our own mortality is but a fleeting care.

For in the garden of our souls, where memories take root,
Your beauty blooms anew, a flower of eternal fruit,
Unbound by time and space, your essence spreads like light,
Illuminating paths we've walked, banishing the darkest night.

And when we gaze upon your beauty, lost and gone from sight,
We're reminded of our own mortality's fleeting light,
And though our own existence is but a brief, shining spark,
In your immortal beauty, we find solace in the dark.

So let us cherish every moment, every fleeting glance,
Every whispered promise of your ephemeral dance,
For in your transience, we find the beauty that remains,
And in your immortality, the love that sustains.

VI

I stand upon the earth, a fleeting thought,
A moment's breath, a heartbeat's length, and I'm naught.
Yet, beneath my feet, ancient secrets sleep,
In rocks that weather, worn, yet still keep.
Their stories whispered, etched in stone and time,
Of eons past, when seas and mountains aligned.
The winds of ages have shaped and worn,
Leaving tales of lives that rose and mourned.
In granite's heart, a fire still burns bright,
A spark that glows, though civilizations take flight.
In quartz's clear depths, the memories remain,
Of crystals formed, in ancient, mystic rain.
I think of all that's passed, and all that's yet to be,
And realize that rocks are all I'll see.
For as I stand, a moment's pause, a breath,
They remain, steadfast, through life's brief death.
In their enduring silence, I find peace,
A reminder that some things will never cease.
For in the stillness of their ancient hearts,
I find a solace that will never depart.
Their immortality speaks to me of more,
Of lives that flow like rivers to the shore.
Of moments lived, and moments lost, yet preserved,
In stones that whisper secrets of the universe.
And so I stand upon this earth,
With rocks beneath my feet, and eternal truth.
For in their timeless wisdom, I find my own,
A fleeting thought, yet grounded in the stone.

VII

As I sit here, lost in thought's grey sea,
I ponder the stream's immortality.
A life that flows, yet never grows old,
A constant flow, as the seasons unfold.
Like life itself, it ebbs and it flows,
With twists and turns, as the years go by.
Yet, despite its course, so winding and slow,
It remains, steadfast, through all the ages' toll.
The waters that pass, like memories fade,
Yet the stream's essence remains, unbroken and stayed.
Like our own stories, of love and of strife,
The stream's tale unwinds, a continuous thread of life.
Just as our souls, like ripples on the lake,
Reflect the world's turmoil, and our own heart's ache,
The stream's surface mirrors life's turbulent ride,
Yet beneath its depths, a calm and peaceful tide.
Through times of drought, and seasons of rain,
The stream perseveres, an eternal refrain.
Unchanging and true, like the heart's own beat,
The stream's immortal flow, our own mortality meets.
In its endless flow, I find a sense of peace,
A reminder that our own lives will cease.
Yet in the stream's eternal flow, I find solace too,
For though our moments pass, its story is forever anew.
So let us cherish the fleeting moments we share,
And find solace in the stream's unbroken care.
For though we are mortal, like the waters we pour,
The stream's immortality reminds us of life's eternal roar.

VIII

As I stand on the mountain's height,
I feel the wind's gentle, persistent might.
It whispers secrets, ancient and old,
Of lives lived, loves lost, and stories untold.
In its sighs, I hear the whispers of the past,
Echoes of laughter, tears, and moments vast.
The wind remembers all that's been and gone,
A keeper of memories, forever strong.
It blows through cities, where steel and stone prevail,
And rustles through forests, where life's pulse fails.
It carries the scent of blooming flowers,
And whispers tales of distant, forgotten hours.
Though I am mortal, finite and brief,
The wind remains eternal, forever relief.
It dances with the trees, a waltz so free,
A reminder that some things are meant to be.
In its immortality, I find a peace,
A sense that some things will never cease.
The wind's breath is a balm to my soul,
A reminder that some things are forever whole.
So let me listen to its gentle sigh,
And let its whispers carry me to the sky.
For in its eternal breath, I find a sense of peace,
A reminder that some things are truly immortal release.

IX

Rain's eternal dance, a waltz of time
A celestial rhythm, forever aligned
With earth's own pulse, it beats and sways
A symphony of life, in endless ways
As I stand beneath its whispering hush
I'm reminded of the secrets it has clutch
The memories of ages past, now gray
Yet in its drops, a story's told anew each day
It's been the witness to humanity's rise
And falls, and all the moments that we've prized
From ancient civilizations to modern strife
The rain has seen it all, yet still remains in life
It's washed away the tears of sorrow and pain
And quenched the thirst of love and joy's sweet refrain
It's shaped the earth and molded mountains high
A testament to nature's enduring sigh
And though I'm mortal, fleeting as a sigh
The rain remains, a constant in the sky
A reminder that some things will never fade
A beauty that endures, long after I've been made
So let me bask in its eternal rain
And let my spirit soar, like a bird that's not in vain
For in its rhythmic beat, I hear a gentle voice
Whispering secrets of the ages, a reminder of life's choice.

X

Like me, you've seen it all, dear river,
From dawn's first light to twilight's hush.
Your waters flow, a constant stream,
While I, like life itself, am but a fleeting dream.
Your banks have cradled civilizations past,
And witnessed the rise and fall of empires vast.
You've carried secrets of the earth below,
And borne the weight of humanity's ebb and flow.

Yet, still you flow, unbroken and serene,
A testament to life's enduring sheen.
Your currents whisper ancient tales untold,
Of seasons' cycles, growth and decay to mold.
As I stand on your banks, I feel the weight
Of time's passage, marked by life's brief fate.
But you, dear river, know no end or bounds,
Your eternal flow, a dance of life's profound.
Your waters merge with those that came before,
A lineage of stories, forever in store.
In your depths, I see the wisdom of the ages,
A reflection of my own mortality's pages.
Yet, in your immortality, I find solace too,
For in your endless journey, I see my own path anew.
Though I may fade like autumn's leaves or winter's snow,
You'll flow on, a reminder of life's eternal glow.
So here I'll stand, and let your waters wash
Over my feet, and soothe my troubled past.
For in your eternal flow, I find a sense of peace,
A reminder that some things endure, and never cease.

XI

As I stand here, bathed in golden light,
I ponder the fleeting nature of life.
The sun, a constant in my mortal sight,
Shines bright, yet I know it too will take flight.
I've seen the seasons come and go,
Bringing with them the joys and woes.
I've felt the warmth of summer's breath,
And shivered through the icy winter's death.
But amidst this cycle of life and decay,
The sun remains, a beacon of eternal sway.
It rises each day, unbroken and free,
A reminder that some things are meant to be.
In its radiance, I find solace and peace,
A sense of connection to the universe's release.
For in its light, I see the beauty and might,
Of a power that transcends mortal sight.
Like me, all things must pass and fade,
But not the sun. It shines on, unafraid.
A symbol of hope, a beacon of light,
Guiding us through the darkest of nights.
As I bask in its warmth, I am reminded too,
That even in death, there is still something new.
For in its rays, I see the promise of life,
And know that even mortality is but a brief strife.
So let us cherish this gift from above,
This eternal radiance that brings us love.
For in its light, we find our way,
Through the trials and tribulations of each passing day.

XII

The birds that sing their sweet refrain,
Their songs a symphony of joy and pain.
Their feathers, a gentle hue of blue,
A reflection of the skies they flew.

But as I watch them, with a grown man's eyes,
I see the fleeting nature of their lives.
A flash of life, a burst of song,
And then, they're gone, their stories gone.

Their mortality, a stark reminder,
Of the brevity of human life.
For though we soar, though we may glide,
Our wings are bound, our fate is tied.

But still we dream, we hope, we pray,
To break free from our earthly sway.
To live forever, like the birds that fly,
Free from the chains of mortality's sigh.

And so we chase the wind, we chase the sun,
We chase the dreams that have just begun.
For though we're mortal, though we're bound,
Our spirits soar, our hearts unbound.

The birds that sing their sweet refrain,
Their songs a symphony of joy and pain.
They remind us to live in the moment,
To cherish every breath, every fleeting instant.

So let us cherish these feathered friends,
These birds that live, and then again begin.
Let us learn from their resilience,
From their ability to thrive in adversity.

For though we're mortal, though we're bound,
Our spirits soar, our hearts unbound.
And in the end, it's not the length of our lives,
But the depth of our love, our laughter and our tears.

The birds that sing their sweet refrain,
Their songs a symphony of joy and pain.
They remind us to live, to love and to give,
To cherish every moment, every breath we live.

XIII

The land, a canvas old and worn,
A testament to time's unyielding scorn,
It stands, a sentinel, unmoved and gray,
While mortal dreams and empires fade away.

I've walked its paths, and seen the rise,
Of civilizations that touched the skies,
Their triumphs, failures, and grand design,
Leaving behind only echoes of a bygone line.

But as I stand, and gaze upon its face,
I see the secrets hidden in its ancient space,
The stories of the earth, the whispers low,
Of lives lived long ago, and long since gone.

And yet, despite the passage of time's hand,
The land remains, a constant in this land,
Unchanging, steadfast, and true of heart,
A reminder of the impermanence we play our part.

I've seen the seasons come and go, each year,
Bringing with it life, and death, and tears,
The wind that whispers through its ancient trees,
And the rain that weeps upon its weathered knees.

And yet, the land remains, untouched and still,
A testament to time's immortal will,
For in its depths, I see the memories of old,
And know that though we pass, the land remains to hold.

The land is a reflection of our own fate,
A reminder that our lives are but a fleeting state,
For though we may be born, and live, and die,
The land remains, a constant in the sky.

And so I stand, and look upon its face,
And know that though my time may be but a fleeting space,
The land remains, a constant and true friend,
A reminder of the impermanence that we must contend.

XIV

In the depths of my being, a secret lies
A truth that whispers to me, as I gaze to the skies
A reminder of life's fleeting nature, yet
A testament to endurance, a tale of ancient allure

The earth beneath my feet, a canvas so old
A testament to the passing of time, stories untold
The soil that nourishes all life, a story to share
A tale of birth, growth, decay, and rebirth, forever there

I think of all that has been lost and gained
The memories that have faded, like the morning's dew-stained
The laughter and tears, the triumphs and fears
Yet, amidst the turmoil, the soil remains, unwavering and clear

It's a reminder of the fleeting nature of our existence
A poignant truth that we must confront and confess
For in the face of mortality, it stands tall and proud
A symbol of resilience, an eternal foundation unbound

Like the ancient trees that stand sentinel around
The soil that cradles their roots, a story to be found
Of seasons come and gone, of storms and sun's rays
Yet still it remains, unchanged, a steadfast heart that beats

In this fleeting world, where life is but a brief span
The soil stands as a witness, a testament to life's plan
A reminder of our connection to this land we call home
A bond that binds us all, like threads in a tapestry sewn

So let us cherish this earth, this soil that gives us life
And honour its ancient wisdom, its enduring strife
For in its depths, we find our roots, our foundation so strong
A reminder of our immortality, where life begins anew.

XV

1

I wander through the forest deep,
Where trees whisper secrets in their sleep.
The creatures here, they dance and play,
Their laughter echoing through the day.

The flowers bloom, the birds take flight,
The sun shines down with all its might.
But sometimes, I see things that scare,
Like dying leaves and empty air.

The forest's magic is so strong,
It makes me feel like I belong.
But when I think of all that's gone,
I wonder if it's time to move on.

Is this forest mortal, like me?
Will it fade away, like a leaf on a tree?
Or is it immortal, like a dream?
Will it live forever, in a world unseen?

I'll keep exploring, day by day,
And learn the secrets of this forest's way.
And maybe someday, I'll find the key,
To unlock its secrets, and set its magic free.

2

In the twilight of existence, I stand

Among the shadows of a dying land.
The forest's pulse is weak and slow,
As if its very lifeblood was draining low.

The ancient trees, they whisper tales,
Of seasons past, and distant gales.
Their wisdom echoes through the night,
As I behold the fleeting light.

In this fleeting moment, I behold
The cycle of life, where all is told.
From birth to death, and rebirth anew,
The ecosystem's eternal truth shines through.

Yet, in this ephemeral world of ours,
Lies hidden an eternal force that endures.
A thread of life that weaves and binds,
Connecting all that is, and all that will be aligned.

In this dance of life and death, I find
A glimpse of eternity intertwined.
For even as the mortal world decays,
The ecosystem's essence remains in eternal sway.

Let these echoes of eternity remain,
As testament to life's eternal refrain.
And though our mortal forms may fade away,
The forest's essence will forever stay.